Verses

OF A

WOUNDED SUN

UDAY S. BHADORIYA

To my father,
who taught me strength in silence.
To my mother,
whose quiet endurance shaped my soul.
This book is my offering.

CONTENTS

From the world of 'Cheeku'

From the world of 'Healed'

FOREWORD

There are friendships, and then there are kinships born not of blood, but of battles -- some we've fought together, and some within ourselves. Uday and I share the latter. He is not just a friend; he is a brother knitted into the folds of my life like a second heartbeat, a co-conspirator in creation and, at times, in destruction. We've held each other up when the nights were long and the world quieter than it should be. And so, when he asked me to write this foreword, I didn't feel honoured, I felt entrusted. Because to introduce Verses of a Wounded Sun is not to speak about a book, but to speak of a soul.

Uday is one of those rare people who can sit with you in silence and still say something profound. The kind of person who, if you called him at 2 a.m., would not only answer, but bring with him words that heal, unsettle, and provoke. As a writer, he is fluent in pain and grace, unafraid of turning himself inside out if it helps someone else. His craft isn't polished for perfection, it's raw for resonance. And that's precisely why this book doesn't read like poetry but it bleeds like memory.

Verses of a Wounded Sun is a map of scars that so many of us carry but never name. I didn't just read this book, I recognized myself in it. Somewhere in the cracks of its verses, in the breath between its stanzas, I saw reflections of my own confusion, rage, tenderness, and longing. There's something profoundly personal about these pages yet they are spacious enough to hold your own griefs and dreams too.

If I had to name a favourite section and it's not easy, I'd say Cheeku moved me the most. "To the Little bro" and "An Apology Letter" in particular felt like pages torn from my own unspoken chapters. They aren't just poems; they are conversations we wish we had, the ones that linger long after the door has closed. They remind us of the little boys we once were, of the men we are still trying to become, and of the soft, difficult love that hides behind every apology we couldn't voice in time.

This book is not meant to be consumed in a single sitting. It's meant to be carried like a secret, like a wound, like a truth you're not yet ready to say out loud. It's for the readers who have written their own verses in the margins of notebooks they'll never show anyone. For those who've ever had to grow up too fast, love too deeply, or feel too much. For the broken, the healing, and the unapologetically alive.

To anyone picking up Verses of a Wounded Sun, know this: you're not alone. These pages will sit with you in your solitude. They will ask difficult questions and refuse easy answers. But more than anything, they will remind you that even the most wounded sun still rises and sometimes, that rising looks a lot like writing. So here it is: not just a book, but a mirror.

Welcome to Uday's world. It might just feel like yours too.

Shivam Jha

(Columnist, Legal Researcher & Law Student)

31st May 2025

PREFACE

I have been writing for a long, long time– close to a decade, if I were to count. In the beginning, I believed that storytelling was where my strength lay. Then came poetry– slowly, unexpectedly, and I found myself drawn to it, not just as a form of expression, but as something I could do well. I say that without arrogance, only with the quiet confidence of someone who has lived with his words long enough to see where they come from.

For a long time, I carried a fear– the fear of being judged. In a society where men are rarely encouraged to speak of their feelings, let alone write about them, I worried: *What would happen if the world discovered my poems?* To share them felt like standing bare-chested in front of a crowd: exposed, vulnerable, fragile.

And then, life brought me in touch with some of the finest individuals I've ever met, people who were not only rich in intellect but also in emotion. Some of them became my mentors, and through their unwavering belief in me, a belief stronger than my own, they nudged me forward. They didn't just encourage me to write; they helped me find my voice, and gave it a direction.

Over time, I gathered the courage to take their advice seriously. I sat down, looked back, and began compiling the verses I had written– many recently, some over the years. I've always had the habit of writing poems in sets and not isolated pieces, but fragments of a larger narrative. I've rarely thought in terms of a single emotion or moment; my poems tend to tell stories, weaving together reality and metaphor, wounds and wonder.

Now, I believe the time has come, the time to let this book breathe in the open. And in doing so, I have perhaps overcome my greatest fear: the fear of being vulnerable, of being truly seen

Uday S. Bhadoriya

3rd May 2025

INTRODUCTION

This book is not merely a collection of poems. It is a journey through emotion, memory, and becoming. Divided into three thematic sets – *Crestfallen*, *Cheeku*, and *Healed* – each section captures a distinct phase of internal experience.

The first set, **Crestfallen**, explores the battles we fight within ourselves. These are poems about darkness, guilt, confusion, and fleeting moments of warmth amidst chaos. Sometimes we lose sight of who we are, sometimes we dwell in what we've lost, and other times we cling to brief memories of joy. This set reflects the turbulence of identity and the quiet suffering that rarely shows.

The second set, **Cheeku**, is personal in every sense. If I had to describe it in one line, it would be: a surge of identity. These poems follow a thread of growth from confusion to clarity, from boyhood to a fragile sense of selfhood. It is a journey of becoming, shaped by existential questions and anchored by two pillars of my life: my father, whose silence influenced me deeply, and my mother, whose quiet strength never left my side.

The final set, **Healed**, does not speak of perfect healing. It speaks of scars that remain, no longer aching visibly, but still present beneath the surface. These poems question meaning, reflect on the past, and slowly lead into a kind of rebirth. Not an answer, but an acceptance. A reminder that tomorrow is tomorrow, and what we truly have is today.

This book is an offering of feeling. Each poem holds a fragment of what I could not speak aloud. If you find yourself somewhere in these lines, know that you were meant to.

From the world of...

'Crestfallen'

– A battle of existence

1

Do you Believe in God? (Prologue)

Do you believe in god?
- I don't know, never thought that way

Do you believe that he exists?
- I guess so

So you believe in those epics?
- I do, I believe in the ideas, I believe in the cause though I'm not pretty sure what they say has happened or not but I'm sure about one thing – that god is no history, history is past, past is evil. I think he is omniscient, he is omnipresent. He says pray to the power not to the picture, pray for the greater good.

And Who is He?
- He is inception, he is the end, in fact He is You and I'm Him, He is life, he is death also and I'm not manifesting these things he said these himself. Though I believe that what he meant remained cryptic all these years everyone formed their own opinions and that's fine but

somewhere I believe what he was trying to say was – to love and care things around you, to love your own self, to be kind to others

That means your god is different? He isn't Religious?
- My god? Isn't he yours too? Why do it always have to look the way that religion is evil? no, it is not it is the way of life, the way I'm grateful to be part of and I'm sure others are too. In bringing religion to the forefront we tend to forget, *people are evil.*

Last thing, what do you think is god?
- I am.

2

At the Doorstep

Slumbering in like a death-made bed
Sanity scrawled where my doormat bled.
At the threshold stood a boy, unshod–
I welcomed him. He laughed like a god.

He claimed he brought some friends along,
"Fear not, my mirth does no man wrong."
All he asked for was a reckless spree–
For I was idle, drowned in ennui.

They laid their burdens on my floor,
We drank stale milk and begged for more.
To broken souls, a silent toast!
We mocked the weak, we praised the ghost.

A symposium of sorts, like Greeks of old,
We jested bold, we bartered gold.
We cheated fate, hid cards with flair
In his scarf, my shawl–truth laid bare.

We slipped on spilled mango shake
Our sole misstep, a minor quake.

He grinned and handed me a book,
Said he must go, gave one last look:
    "I never linger, I never stay–
So drink me up, then cast me away.
Seek the 'Luke' within, or let him die,
And rise a 'Kylo' with fire in eye."

    The book was bound in sleepless ink,
And came with a letter that made me think.
It stirred a storm of silent vice,
Renounce the three: sweet, spice, and vice.

    "Embrace your madness, call it art–
Wrestle your daemon, tear it apart.
Don't seek salvation in sugar and lies–
Burn through your crises. Be what won't die."

3

Existential Crisis

I had three best friends.
Two dissolved into time – unknown ends.
But one... he returns without grace or track.
He keeps coming back.
He keeps coming back.

No matter how often I cast him away,
Exile him with silence, or lead him astray
He clings like fate in a forgotten myth.
I beg him to go,
Yet he tightens his grip.
Once, I crowned him my strongest shield
Now I see the sword he wields.
The betrayal quiet, but complete
He won't retreat.

Anger. Resentment. Fear.
Phantom brothers that disappear.
Two are ghosts, I hear no sound.
But Anger still circles, close and profound.
The crest is slipping,
I am crestfallen.

His footsteps echo,
And still, he's calling.

    I can't open every door inside
The chambers echo, vast and wide.
I fell apart with no war cry sung,
No Post Malone, just a silent tongue.
    An existential burn, unnoticed flame,
A slow decay with no name.
Why must I ache with these notions' war,
Where answers drip, but truth is shoreless lore?

    Why does he make my breath so heavy
Chains of memory, thoughts unsteady?
I beg him now, I plead below:
"I don't want to know you.
Let me go.
Let me go."

4

Ten Seconds

Butterflies fluttered in my head,
A quiet storm pressed against my chest.
I hadn't known I was a bird myself
Until I saw my resting nest.
She was smiling - subtle, divine
In the backseat of her moving shrine.
And I, caught mid-breath, became
A sapodilla – sweet, shy, unnamed
Half-uncovered, half-concealed,
As if my truth had been softly peeled.

For a moment, I was unsure,
Insecure in the purest way.
I wished no eyes could meet her then,
As she tied her hair in shades of day.
There she was 'this wild thing'
Binding her freedom in a tender swing.
She made it a ponytail, a gentle decree;
I almost knelt, not out of chivalry,
But because that's what you do, I guess,
When you meet the queen of your quiet distress.

It lasted only ten seconds, maybe less,
But ten seconds of sheer aliveness,
Where time itself seemed to hesitate
She tore through my doubt like fate,
Like antihistamines calming a storm,
Like sunlight touching skin still warm.

I don't know if it was *her* I loved,
Or the ache of the passing scene
But those ten seconds were carved in me,
Like verses whispered in a dream.
And I still find myself hoping,
In silence, soft and serene
To witness that again
The moment she sets her hair free.

5

Long Long Day

It felt like snow in mid-July
The way humans do cry
Awful, disheartening & devastated
At a funeral sight
It felt like terrible play
It felt like a long long day

Waiting in harmony, Tearing my agony
All for a text which didn't arrive, quite funny

Seconds into minutes
Minutes into hours
Stood very rigorous for a person
Who devours
Then hours into days
Days into week
No hope prevails
I turned bleak

The day was still vital
Sun was glowing to its brightest
Adjacent to the pond of greed
I saw a gleaming seed

It felt it was calling out to me
For me being a hypocrite
For me being some bad
Bottom to all these evils
It saw me seemingly sad

"I showed me mercy of being assassinated
time and again, though it caused some pain
But at least I stood by myself in those blame rains"

Sun purposely strike me in the eyes
To make - what was' to what lies'
It is never late if you realise
Fake truth, real lies
Months, Years or whatever you may say
But eventually I realised it's just a long long day.

6

Mushroom

The day was still vital
Sun was glowing to its brightest
Adjacent to the pond of greed
I saw a gleaming seed
It felt it was calling out to me
For me being a hypocrite
For me being a sheepish
Apart from all these trifles
Saw me not saying what I wished

It was unique, stand apart
Seemingly harder than the flowers
But still playing its part

The part to make you, you among it
No curtains,
The things you pertain
as your being
just as it is, un-inverted
With its one gaze and some persistent thoughts
of thine
I saw it like it meant to be

no glitters, no shine

a proverb says 'see the mirror'
meaning to see thyself truly
here my eyes are enough when I'm with her
I love the cold and she felt like woolly
The place where I turn to mush
And leave no room
for the inner demons
and push'em to their doom

the long day seems to be over now
Inner conflicts yet to be ploughed
Accept the kind, surrender despise
from the ashes as Phoenix rise

7

Under the wisteria

I got nine lives
But wanna live in this one
tired of those yellow signs
wanna give you crimson
I saw you the other day passing by
You didn't catch a gaze forget about a 'hi'
surface slipped through, looming sky
the alarm buzzed and I took a sigh
of relief, of non zero belief
I assured me, and kept it brief

I periodically see bridges in my vision
can't visualise the sentimental fission
so I had an idea which I kept to myself
but saying seems a side vis on

I know it sounds merrier
let's sit under the wisteria
it would be hard to find it
however, affection won't mind it
how about I...
make you a cup of tea?
we will set our insecurities free

with your song playing
we will hum together like bees

dusk will set us free
and its rays sparkle us like a tree
I know trees don't sparkle
but you'll be startled
sounds great, the cafeteria
but there is something you won't regret
under the wisteria.

8

A poem, close to my heart

2 a.m. sharp, it struck my chest–
A silent ache that broke my rest.
I reached for the pen, no second thought,
To write a verse my heart had sought.
Joy tiptoed in, so full and wide,
Even Happiness turned green with pride.
Sleep, betrayed, sat on the floor,
Murmuring, *"He doesn't need me anymore."*

Love, long used to heartbreak lines,
Now felt adored, between these rhymes.
For once, this wasn't pain in prose–
It was a cake baked warm with all my soul.
Ink, impatient, tried to flood
One single word with all its blood.
I hushed it soft, "Not now, not fast,
This isn't like the poems of past."
There were memories, some still raw,
Some being built without a flaw.
With someone who just broke the rules,
No checks or balances, no bookish tools.

By 2:15, a tide had spun–
A hundred thoughts, and not just one.
My hand froze mid-line, refused to play,
Sighed, *"You've failed to shape this every day."*
    "Another draft? Another try?"

Sleep laughed nearby with half-shut eye.
Like a toddler grinning with a coin,
Mocking how I re-anoint.
    I tossed a pillow at her face,
Said, *"Go sulk in your lazy place."*
But Hope and Love, they stayed in sight,
Whispering, *"Try once more tonight."*

At four o'clock, Sleep stretched again,
Effort growled, "Stop spreading pain.
If you must rest, go out and snore–
Don't block the door with tired decor."
    Sleep snapped back, "What's left to do?
These aren't puzzles, they're inside you.
Stop chasing shape–just speak your part!
The moon will tell the sun your heart."
    I sat there torn, the words unsure,
Love stared on–so soft, so pure.
"You're full of it, yet lost for phrase–
How can you not know what to say?"

And then at five, a knock–too light.
He stepped inside, still wrapped in night.
"Still up? Not slept at all?" he frowned.
Even Sleep grew quiet, fear unbound.

I lied–"Just studying, that's all."
He scoffed, "You'll stumble when you fall.
You'll miss your run. Don't waste the day."
I kept the pen. I looked away.
For that day, I let silence win,
The poem stayed unread within.

They say daughters write with silent ease,
While sons must decode love through pleas.
We tinker, twist, invent our tricks–
To dodge the weight emotions fix.
But every son, in heart or mind,
Wants just one hug, one sacred time–
To hold him close and say with grace,
I love you, Papa. Face to face.
Yet most of us–too scared to start–
Keep waiting for the perfect part.

Father–a word of iron and earth,
A lifetime's labor, silent worth.
A thousand feelings, masked with grit,
With dusty hands, and brows sweat-lit.
And once again, I failed to show
The poem that he'll never know–
The one I hold so close, yet part,
a poem close to my heart.

9

~~Life~~ Ride Lesson.

Have you ever, oddly enough, grown fond of a feeling rooted in fear?
Strange, I know.
But that's exactly how it felt–learning to drive with my father. every nervous twitch of mine met with two sharp scoldings, sometimes even before the mistake had a chance to happen. It was as if he could sense hesitation before it even surfaced.

They say great writers don't rely on hearsay.
They write what they've lived–what has sunk deep into their soul. And just like that, what was meant to be a driving lesson turned out to be something much more profound. A lesson in life, in patience, in endurance.

There was only one lesson, and truth be told, one was enough. I never had the courage to sit beside him again while driving. Those few minutes behind the wheel felt more demanding than any existential crisis I've endured since.

But with time– and time always knows best– I realised that certain moments aren't meant to be pleasant or easy as they are meant to shape you. They're not always enjoyable while they happen, but later, when you reflect, you understand how essential they were. As he would say, *"Dheere se accelerator lo agar jhatke nahi khana. Jab seekh jaoge, tab hard start le sakte ho."* Little did I know, he wasn't just talking about driving.

He was talking about life.
It's not about rushing ahead.
It's about starting–carefully, intentionally.
And sometimes,
that's all it takes–
a single ride,
close to your heart.

10

Hate/Kill Thy Neighbour

There's a certain stillness in sorrow, a paralysis that traps you in your own skin. You feel the weight of your own heart, yet your body remains unmoved, as though you've been buried alive beneath the weight of your emotions. Meanwhile, I am not still. I am violence in motion. I strike—fists pounding against walls, against a world that feels just as hollow as the spaces I hit. It's an aggression that has no reason but is born from the lack of one. Punch after punch, and I feel nothing but the reverberation of impact, an echo of what is missing inside of me.

I've kept the moon for myself, a silent, cold beauty that no one else can touch. I gave you the sun, as if I were some kind of martyr–offering the only thing of warmth I had, without asking for anything in return. But the moment you dared to question my integrity, to scratch at the surface of my devotion, I saw you for what you were: a threat to the balance I had built in my solitude. I didn't call it betrayal. I called it treason. You were no longer a person in my eyes, but something that had to be silenced.

My hands are torn from the force, the blood already dry, but it's not the blood that bothers me. It's my mind that grows heavy, that grows weaker with each passing moment. You can wound the body and feel pain, but it's the mind that carries the scars that never heal. There will come a time, a moment when I will cease to hear the voice in my head–the one that tells me not to kill, not to destroy, not to erase. The day I no longer listen to it will be the day I am no more. And maybe that's the freedom I seek: to kill the part of me that still clings to morality, that still begs for compassion.

I have often wondered how it feels to take a life. People speak of it like it is an unthinkable act, but when you are driven by the abyss within you, it feels like a release. To take someone's life, to snuff out their existence, doesn't feel like violence–it feels like the universe reordering itself, placing you in a position of godhood, where the consequence of life and death is no longer yours to question. Killing, when done right, feels like the fulfilment of a prophecy, an execution of something far greater than personal vengeance. It is not murder. It is destiny.

So avoid me when I am in a bad mood. Don't speak to me. Don't look at me. I will take what you offer–your pity, your fragility–and I will turn it into nothing. I will carve you open, leave your remains for the world to witness, and never glance back at the carnage I've left behind. It's a cleansing. It's necessary. It's the only truth I can cling to.

I keep two lists, though I don't expect anyone to understand them. The first list is for those who have served me, who have lifted me when I could not stand. They are the ones who know me as I was meant to be known. The second list is for those I have broken, those who crossed me, those who dared to challenge what I had built. I will tell the world about them, but I will also make sure the world knows what they did to deserve what came next.

I've realised something about love and hate. They are not opposites, not in the way the world wants you to believe. Love is a sickness, a weakness that makes you vulnerable, open to the wounds others may inflict. Hate is its cure. Hate is a force that clears away the filth of the world, sharpens the mind, and rips away everything that isn't true. It is as pure as love could never be.

11

Crestfallen

I got bitter
Since I let me down
Moving a step freely
In a world full of pawns.
Am I the only one
Who gets emotionally attached
To broken chapters
And fictional characters?
Why did you do this to me?
Why you?
I know I'm dubious to me–
I do.

We were happy kids, now sad faces
Shining out in bad phases,
Laughter turned to practiced smiles,
Love lost in digital miles.
We stitched dreams
With trembling hands,
Now threads unravel–
And no one understands.

Songs don't sound the same anymore,

Rooms echo more than they store.
Eyes search for what they once knew,
But mirrors reflect a version untrue.
I'm not seeking healing–
Just a pause
Where the heart isn't questioned
For every loss.

And maybe, just maybe,
In the fall,
There's a trace of grace
Left after all.

12

Phoenix (Epilogue)

They thought I was fire. But fire is fleeting–warm, bright, gone. I was the furnace. I was the place where things are broken to be remade, or simply broken beyond repair. I didn't grow into this. I was carved, layer by layer, by silence, by betrayal, by being buried again and again with the expectation that I would stay buried.

There came a point when I stopped asking for help and started listening to what was left inside me after everything else had gone quiet. It wasn't peace. It wasn't healing. It was something older. Something sharp and still breathing.

They called me a hero once–because it was easier to romanticise survival than to look at what it cost. Because if I stopped playing along, if I stopped smiling and started speaking in the voice I found in the dark, they wouldn't know what to do with me. If I turned, truly turned, they'd run out of names for me.

I don't die. Not in the way they think. I decay. I fall apart slowly and in public, and then I gather the pieces. Not all of them. Just the ones that still matter. I burn the rest.

Someone once told me—half in jest, half in warning—"Let loose your fur. Channel the evil. Unfurl Lucifer." I did not need to become evil. I needed to stop pretending I wasn't angry. I needed to stop mistaking obedience for morality. I did not want revenge. I wanted to stop apologising for surviving the way I did.

There is no poetry in my return. No fanfare, no moment of glory. Just the quiet fact of it. Just the sound of footsteps where there should have been none. The people who thought I was finished don't meet my eyes now. Some pray. Some spit. Some pretend they never saw me fall.

I carry no wings. I have no light to offer. My crown is not forged. It grew there—calcified like bone—after too many blows to the same place. I do not speak in prophecy. I do not ask to be understood. But I remember everything. Every hand that let go. Every time I had to become my own shelter.

This is not a story of resurrection. It's a history of persistence. A quiet, brutal refusal to stay dead. There is no glory here—only grit. Only the knowledge that every time they set me on fire, I came back carrying the smoke.

From the world of...

'Cheeku'

– A surge of identity

13

FM (intro)

Have you seen water boiling?
A point comes when it starts to vaporise–
Soft bubbles rise,
whispers of change
in a world that never stays still.

A boy,
just like that water–
nonchalant, innocent,
far from worldly pleasures,
dancing in his own rhythm,
easy to blend in,
hard to disturb.
He hit many boiling points throughout–
words that scalded,
looks that simmered,
moments that scorched.
And once he vaporised,
he did not float–
he froze.
Condensed into ice.
Solid, quiet, unbothered.
That's not how boiling works–

but let's leave that
for some other quirk.

He became a relic–
an echo in static,
like those old FM radios
we once tuned
to feel less alone.
His joy now plays
in a frequency no one listens to.
Static covers laughter,
and memories are commercials
no one asked for.
Once a mixtape of mischief and melody,
he's now background noise–
you catch him only
when the world slows down
and silence finds you.

You remember him–
not by name,
but by the way
your chest felt warmer
when that one song played
at just the right time.

And maybe that's enough–
To be remembered
not for staying,
but for sounding like home
in a passing moment.

14

To the little bro

Bhadoriya Bhawan,
####, #.#. Road
######### - 28***4
Jhansi

7th July 2010

To the little bro,

How are you? How are Maa and Papa? How is Didi? Hope she is not still crying. Do you still get annoyed by being called cheeku, I believe you do. c'mon that's your pet name you'll make peace with it sooner or later like I did. I'm expecting you have seen the peak of dramas held in an Indian household yet the one that happened in front of your eyes seized your heart, it did mine too.

You need not make a shield of your emotions, that won't help and you gotta lower your temper too. Sometimes you have to stand up and act as the elder child of the family which eventually you will be as one of my favourite poets said, "Age doesn't matter, the one who stands tall in crisis is the elder." (~ उम्र से फर्क नहीं पड़ता, बड़ा वो है जिसने बनके दिखाया है ~) I see you have started taking an interest in poetry though you don't write now I believe you'll do promising. I know you got some anger issues and i will advise that you put that anger in your pen that's the only way as of now to get it under control but you will be just fine with time like i did or may be i am lying a lil bit. anyway hold on tight on those idiots you have just started to sit with, you may not have brother carved by blood but you'll have many carved through trust

There is one thing i did not tell you is probably this letter won't reach you, probably you would have left Bhadoriya Bhawan already when this letter hits the mailbox, probably because i may not want it to reach on time to you and probably i don't want to make amends and want it to happen the exact same way it happened. the way You happened, The way I did! and about me everything is fine here, some existential crisis do come and go but they fade when I think about why I started in the first place.

Life is faring well, learning new things, will see you after thirteen years till then take care of yourself, Didi and Papa, or Maa will do of you all.

Be a Tough Fighter.

With love,
Uday

15

Bluetooth Headset

O little boy–
I know a place.
I still go there,
to remember your face.
Hoping that when you sit,
relaxed in thought,
eight years from now,
you'll feel I never left–just forgot
how to tell you I never moved on
from that rock where you once sat alone.

Don't think I've forgotten you.
I've carried you–through and through–
on tired shoulders,
in the furnace of my heart,
in the weary rhythm of my daily part.
Right on my sleeve, always in sight,
you've lingered in shadows,
you've burned in my fight.

The Bluetooth hums a silent tune,

grooving through our afternoons.
Those anger lessons–
they finally broke through,
quiet storms now whispering true.

Heard you've started to write?
What's with the pen and all that fight?
Weren't you the stubborn kind,
all fists, all flame, no peace of mind?
Just teasing–don't kill the spark,
it's what lit our way in the dark.

Kudos, boy–
for growing from hardheaded
to a prudent son.
Now fill your verses,
wounded sun.
The world awaits a rebel's ink–
a sword that makes tyrants sink,
but don't forget the dandelion too:
a bloom for every scar in you.

Let your sword cut where it must–
let it bleed beauty,
let it earn trust.
Don't just peel through life–
tear it open.
Then pour poems

into every wound left broken.

But when you feel your grip on sanity
start to slip toward vanity–
come.
Come back to the mountains.
There's no arrogance here,
just humility in fountains.
Your words will breathe,
your tongue will bend–
stronger, swifter,
around each end.

And I–
I'll keep returning to this sacred space,
to find you
in the echo of your grace.
Until the day you sit beside me,
not as a child,
but as the man who finally saw–
he was never alone at all.
I'll still be patrolling these silent hills,
to refill my ink,
my soul,
from these silver rills.

Happy writing cheeks.

16

An Apology Letter

Dear Papa,

I'm tired – not just the kind of tired that sleep cures, but the kind that creeps into your bones, the kind that turns breath into burden. You wouldn't want to see your son with his shoulders sagging, spine folded like unfinished prayers, but here I stand, clothed in decency, marching in a procession of good intentions that the world tramples without a second glance. I tried, Papa. I really did. I pushed, I bent, I begged the world to change – to mirror the difference you once dreamed of, not just in me, but in the flesh of this rotting system. But people... they don't change. They wear apathy like armor. They worship comfort over conscience. And I, the fool, kept offering flowers in a land of thorns.

Papa, it breaks me – this being good. Every time I hold out my heart, it's returned in pieces. Every kindness met with cruelty, every smile answered by betrayal. I rise each time, like you taught me, but I rise into another storm, not sunlight. I'm sorry, Papa. I'm falling back into the old skin – the one forged in fury, stitched with stubbornness and laced with the ruthless silence of not caring. The boy who felt nothing. Maa says I am what you once were – fire, not yet forged into form. But you had no guide, no anchor. Still, you broke yourself into a father, into a man who bore storms with silence for Maa, for me. And I... I can barely carry drizzle.

Why did you do it, Papa? Why teach me softness in a world that devours the gentle? Why carve me into a gentleman when the world only respects the sharp edges? I can't breathe here anymore. I'm drowning in the weight of being kind, and yet the old ways aren't shelter either. I am stuck in the middle – a creature not cruel enough to survive, not kind enough to thrive. Forgive me if I fall short of the man you are. Forgive me if I can't smile while being spat upon, if I flinch when I hear the curses whispered behind my back. I know you still carry your wounds without a sound. I know you bleed where no one sees. You suffer too, Papa – but your suffering is dignified, like ancient marble cracking in silence. Mine is loud. Mine is messy. Mine is failing.

I want to be like you. God knows I do. But until that day comes, the world will have to know your son as something else – a name that walks like a wound, a boy caught between the fire he was and the light you wanted him to be.

Yours truly.

17

Batman v Superman

Growing up watching cricket as I inherited it from him, indeed I did.
I formulated an adoration for superheroes too
A thousand times exact if they say they have seen better as a fan
I would nonetheless say the best I saw was -
'Batman V Superman'

It was like he had a part in my love for superheroes at that moment watching something he considered stupid.
He was genuinely into it or he did do it for me?
Anyhow, a new sight of him that I got to see
I can never reciprocate the joy I felt that time
I cannot put adjectives to the emotion so sublime
It was like him reuniting with his heroes that he had put to sleep long back
and I have brought down and dusted that locked box from the rack

He questions me things while we sit to watch cricket

because it is our shared love
Regardless his sharing my love was absurdly
beautiful and bewitching to me
He reminded me of little cheeku annoying him
with his questions when he used to watch the
news
Never have I been so much excited explaining!
Little did he know he was my superhero too.

What's the best feeling in the world?
- To father your father
It's not what the world may contemplate it to
look like
Now and then they want to be our child too
They wanna get involved with us
Even if it includes watching Batman V
Superman with us

Maa scolded both of us as if both of us were her
child, maybe we were.
She forwarded us to do something productive
and stop watching cartoon
Yes!, she doesn't get the difference between live-
action and cartoons
Superheroes are cartoons for her. Period.

We ignored her, We laughed
And we continued...

18

Nothing

All that chaos around turns to hush
When I sit in silence, I think of nothing
I look at the distress around and I think of
nothing

Has there been nothing on my sanity recently or
am I compiling my introspections and calling
them nothing. People are shallow spiritually so
they keep filling that space with every possible bad
to feel good. Infidelity became a criterion so does
mistrust
Real, true, and pure are just mere adjectives to
put on - when I think of love – I think of nothing

What are those noises? why are they deafening?
Deads don't react then why am I baffling?
They say what are you? I think of nothing
I'm an outcome of tiny pieces of many people,
they gave a little of themselves to me
Apart from those pieces, I'm nothing
What do I possess that is all me except this
poetry I think of nothing

There have been a cosmos of thoughts that I
knit regularly, I see things and intentions, I see
through people; I know their teachers, I know
their disciples
The dirt behind their white collars
I know all those sent maulers
I think plenty - about escaping reality, about
time travel, about you, about every slight thing
that matters to the world
Is it a boon? Or curse that'll bring doom?
Either of it, I think of nothing

My 'nothing' comprises of my world
They keep on asking,
What are you thinking?
when I think of you I say 'nothing'.

19

A few poems

There are constantly three stages to a man's life – Love, Acceptance, and Progressing on. there were some poems to this life too

If I recall, She was a poem too!
Dear to me but painful
Called her my sunshine
And she put me in the darkest phase of my life

"What would you do for love?"
– Nothing, I'm exhausted, coming from a lineage of fire turned Cold, frosted!

The second poem I was writing
was half-hearted fighting
To write, and the pen broke in the middle
reminding me to not commit to verses fiddle
with shivering hands
With backspacing wands
I always had hesitation while writing a poem
Result in me continually failing to start satisfactory
Still, I have reached so far by reading it
The impulse in me to write is long steered

But I saw the exact guilelessness I had back then
on her face when a string of her hair cleared

    Considering it I may write a new poem
Contrary to devastation, it will be nonchalant,
Innocent, will provide peace and ease to the gazes
Might have already sat down to pen a few verses

    But, The opening of this poem reminds me of
the first few verses of the first poem I wrote
though the person writing it has developed
However, in the end, the author rot
    Reminds me of the gambler who knowingly that
it's for no good of his to gamble but still goes for it
anyway

I feel..
She is a poem too!
unread to me but serene.

20

A Walking Miracle

She ain't no sunshine
She is the dawn of death
Tying her bun, wrecking wrath
She ain't no perfume
Just pure crystal meth
A walking moncor wearing a hat
Thick thighs, brown eyes
No, I don't ask for much
Crushing me in her arms
Sealing my lips, making me hush

I can go on describing you for an eternity
the goddess of love is from your fraternity

God wielded lava in his pen composing you
at least I should afford to burn a few – pages
on which I'll put you down in words
add metaphors as many as boys in herd
after you, this may sound absurd
but you leave everyone blurred
Giving them existential crisis
Or a hope to survive life and fight it

Her name spelt *m i r a c l e*
evening to feel, morning she seems

Some day I will compile my ballads
With a little teal and some beige palettes
It will have loss at first
& mourning on the last page
peace in between which is you
in rest all page

21

Nightmares (Bridge)

I was always a difficult child, or so they said
not in violence, no, not in temper, but in silence,
in the art of becoming a fortress. Not a castle to be
admired, but a stone wall with no doors, moss
growing over forgotten bricks,
where no one dared knock, and I never called out.
I was stubborn, yes. Pretentious, perhaps.
But what else is one to do when the skin you wear
is a costume sewn from what people expect of
you? They saw a nice boy, slightly irritating at
times a harmless, well-spoken ghost of politeness
but I was not there. I had long since moved into
the attic of myself, where even the mirrors lie and
the light is just a memory from a window I
boarded shut.

I never had the courage to present myself the
real one, the trembling, fractured image behind
my eyes that asked, daily: *What if they don't love
you? What if they see you, really see you, and walk
away?"* I have always feared that truth more than
death, because death ends pain, but this... this is
living in rejection's echo, again and again, like

being dragged through a hallway of closed doors where each handle bears your name but none open–not anymore.

Solitude became a kind friend, not because it embraced me, but because it never turned away. In silence, I didn't have to perform. I didn't have to risk. I didn't have to hear someone say, *"No, this version of you is not acceptable."* If someone close, someone I called *mine*, looked me in the eye and recoiled, what would be left of me? My entire edifice would crumble and I, like some Kafkaesque insect, would lay twitching under the weight of their contempt, unrecognisable even to myself. And the dreams–no, *not* dreams. They are nightmares, and they do not wait for sleep. They walk with me in daylight, whispering catastrophes through the smallest cracks in my confidence.

What if I fail? What if, one day, I am struck down and the spirit to rise again has rotted in the cellar of my being? What if I let go of the strings holding me upright, drop my shoulders, collapse into a pile of former ambitions? What happens then? I see these scenarios like horror-films every variation where I lose, where I am unloved, where I become nothing more than a burdensome memory in someone's mouth, a whisper of *"he could have been..."* And I cannot bear it. I can bear the hatred of strangers, for they do not know me, and thus they hate a stranger, not *me*. But if *they*– the ones I love–resent who I am, then the horror is not in being misunderstood but in being *understood perfectly* and still abandoned.

That is the truest terror not to be alone, but to be known and then *left*. People speak of failure as if it were a lesson, a phase, a pit one climbs out of. But for me, it is a bottomless place, and every time I near its edge, I feel a pull like gravity whispering, *"This is your home."* There, I do not cry or scream; I merely become still. A breathing corpse of ambition and despair, haunted by the face of every person I failed to make proud.

And maybe, all of this–
my wall, my silence, my refusal to *be*– is just a defence against one inevitable, shattering truth: I am not who I hoped I would be.
I am only this: a mask worn for the comfort of others, afraid to take it off because beneath it there may be nothing worth loving.

22

Guns & Pens

You perhaps haven't seen
the abundance of guns together
that I keep at home
I could have rubbed
your face in blood
like Augustus of Rome

I wasn't bred to obey
I was born to govern
Just it was only two ways
One might, one firm

There was a fight
between Mind & Might
between Pen & Sword
between War & Words
I resorted to those peaceful one
cause I wished to be a great son

Him and I both wanted me to rule
He believed through wisdom,
I intended of might as a tool

He was aware of what catastrophe the guns
could fetch
He handed me a pen and unfolded his life
sketch
The one thing he asked for
was to not repeat his life
It is not a life of pride but arrogance
and throat to the knife

I have seen people exhibiting their firearms
on social platforms
Gradually it is evolving to be a norm
Might have been restricted to those platforms
foremost these days
and the mind has already been consumed by
worms

23

The best two consecutive days so far..

You may have seen the snowball hitting its
lowest during an avalanche
I was that snowball in twenty twenty-one
When nothing was going right
No mercy of God, uncertain plights
It's been a while
Conning smile
Exhibited some courage and asked her out
Immodest me didn't even take counts of her
about
And then I met her after a long being my
sentiments at war
since that instant, I had the best 2 consecutive
days so far...

Commenced with her sitting in front of me
When she set her hair free
Those ten seconds were something I will want
on loop
When the room temperature goes 2° degrees
We listened to my favourite music and stood in
silence

Don't know about her, but looking at her my
mind was playing the violins

Bid her bye, came back home with low
shoulders
    I was feeling heavy as if chained with boulders
    Did she notice that?
    Or I'm just overthinking
    Not many know that I stutter when I get anxious
or excited
    And my breaths go intense
    When did I stutter last, Even I don't have any
reminiscence
    It was her presence that made me anxious
    Still unravelling why is that
    Why does only she do that to me
    Not that I love her or something but there is
something certain under the matt

    As momentarily as I let go of this thought
    Every tiny thing that makes me happy started to
transpire
    That day when I met her and the following one
    were so fortuitous as if someone conspired

    I know nothing like John Snow if I will have
more than one day collectively good at this par
    But I know that these were the best 2
consecutive days so far...

24

Superheroes growing old

Giggling, gazing at them rise
'Soon to be over' days not to my surprise
When they will put their boots off
This thought is enough that shoots up -
panic in my veins
while I'm standing in the rains
empty road and I'm getting drained
drenching joy I see through them

It is for them who i am, what i am
they injected me with courage
infested me with mayhem
the chaos that i seep, with in my veins deep!
they are ones who sowed it
carved a lion outta sheep.
the way i think, i owe to them
traces of me chivalry go to them

I write it then I despise it
I am short of words on some issues
writes 'three superheroes' then hides it
tuck it under bed,
eyes blood red.

anger doesn't get on me nerve these days
it's sadness that rides it

what it hurts? that no efforts!
can turn the inevitable
that could be written in words
my heroes are getting old
those who sold! me ideas of heroics
and some stories untold.

this is a little unconventional to write on it
maybe a letter could do.
have had the idea of writing it so many a times
that actually writing it seems like a deja vu

the ideas behind these 'texts' was to
bring cheeku out
so that I could know him
what he has felt and is today, I could show him

this poem will forever feel like a void
as to eminem, the detroit.
that left me with a fear of not seeing
my heroes at their best again.
it is me that is left to get that mayhem
on my shoulders, infest again!
what i could bring out in words
is because of the ideas!
that were instilled in him
what those heroes filled in him
that he only knew,
'this head doesn't obey gravity

this courage has no knees'
this mentally fucked up kid take no backseat
this madness take no sprees

panic in my veins,
while I'm standing in the rains
that I'm burdened with glorious purpose
never left to be free
i owe my traits and I to my superheroes growing
old –
VK, KK & SSB.

25

Unlove

A girl raised a question to me today "Do you still love her?"

I answered in positive.

I couldn't lie, the exact way I couldn't love someone else since you

Do you desire her back? " she reiterated, to which I responded in negative

She was perplexed at my response, she assumed of I was someone who is not over his past.

But who will tell her that I'm!

Who will tell her that when we burn bridges with our loved ones that don't always mean we stop loving them like we used to

Past is invincible, and can't be wiped off

You are there because I like to keep bad chapters too

I'm eventually at equilibrium with myself, I have acknowledged myself more than anyone, and I have figured out myself better.

But that girl...

Who will tell her that the first and innocent love of mine is lost forever to never be found again,

My care, affection, respect, and concerns never altered for anyone

who will tell her that you departed me with my biggest insecurity of "loving someone and not getting the same love back"

My father taught me to be enraged but he also taught me to be humble and quiet

Just like my mother taught me to love but she never taught me to unlove, how could she? If she knew she would have taught my father to unlove his father first.

Loving you is my second greatest ache after my father's

and this ache will go with me to my pyre

Tomorrow some different girl will inquire me the same but I will lie this time

It's quicker to lie than to unlove.

26

Disdain

Am i ready for this conversation?
I have been running out of patience
agitated, brawled like I'm satan;
this world I live in, I'm hating.
as if tragedies are supposed to find me,
sorrow cuddles me tightly
and disdain surrounds me
am i being the cosmos of accumulation of all the
sob tales? am I the main subject of all the epic
fails?

disdain is over head now
I like less, i despise more
I loved being stupid,
now I'm a deserted folklore
always been the poet, never the poem
it was always them, there was no him
this third person perspective of stories has
disrupted the lore.

I have developed something beyond emotions that
is more brutal, more gore.

how am I supposed to tell that man in the bus that
what he did that day took a living life of a woman?
who is no better than a walking dead.
how am I supposed to start the conversation when
all I saw was regret of twenty years at least that's
what his eyes said.
how am i not to disdain of this human race?
which wakes up and wears a new face
does that one decision of his not broke her life?
does his step to not take him as wife –
killed what was left for her to live.
does the regret I see in his eyes, will ever be
suffice?

I loved stories, I loved them tales
now the very has come to haunt me
all I see is sadness scattered
the tragedies have come to found me
I despise stories, i despise writing
i despise love and the lovers fighting
i despise him and his twenty years of pain
empathy has kicked off & I'm in disdain.

27

Character Arc

Yesterday morning, I woke up, though not with urgency and stood before the mirror as one stands before a judge. And what I saw startled me, not in form, but in essence.

There, staring back, was a man who no longer flared at trivial provocations, Who, curiously, had begun to find more solace in silence than in striving. Something had shifted. No, matured. Hardened, perhaps.

I have begun to learn, I think. Not through books or grand philosophies, but through faces. The kind of faces that speak without pride, that endure without recognition. Faces of those who, by every measure, possess less than I do, And yet carry themselves with such disarming grace, Their smiles unchanged by time or circumstance, Their warmth never once calculated.

How, I ask, can one not be humbled in their presence? – Once, not long ago, I was a creature of pride. Arrogance masked my insecurity, rage my helplessness. I wounded people with my indifference, Though part of me was aware of it– And part of me was too frightened to care.

But was it entirely my fault?
Is a man ever wholly to blame for the temperament that the world itself feeds into him? Or is he merely a vessel, twisted by the heat of circumstance?
Ah, but that's too convenient, isn't it?
The truth is I was molten once, and now I cool. Slowly. In pain. Time, the sculptor of men, is at work within me, and though I do not yet know what I shall become– Stone idol or scattered rubble– I endure the process, Because faith in the process is all that remains when certainty deserts you.

There have been moments, yes! dangerous moments, Where the soul whispers: "Enough. This world is a sham. Humility is weakness. Love is a mask. Kindness is a performance." I have seen hypocrisy wear robes of virtue. I have witnessed cruelty with polished shoes and warm smiles.

What man could remain untouched?

And yet, just when I am on the verge of abandoning all that I have gathered, Some unseen hand, a memory, perhaps, or a thread of conscience, pulls me back.
Back from the brink.
Back to the truth that learning is not linear,
And virtue, though often mocked, is never in vain.

So tomorrow– yes, tomorrow– I shall rise again.
And I shall look into that same mirror,
Not for vanity, but for witness.
And I shall find, perhaps,
That I am a little more patient,
A little more weary, yes, but also a little more resolved.
A little more reconciled with my contradictions.
A little more Uday,
And God willing, a little more human.

28

Reincarnation

I have never seen him like this before.
Not my father.
Not the man who built walls,
not the man whose words were like stones,
whose silence could crush the air around it.
But today, he was only a man.
A man standing in the ruins of something
he did not understand,
a man whose heart seemed to break
not with the force of grief,
but with the absence of something that could
explain it.

He cried.
Not quietly, not with the dignity
that might have made it bearable.
He cried as though the world had unraveled
and he was left clutching at threads,
as though the air itself had betrayed him.
I did not know how to move,
how to walk into the spaces between his sobs
and be something more than a shadow,
more than a passerby

on the edge of something too vast
to comprehend.

He had never needed comfort before.
Not in the ways that the world would teach us–
not in ways that could be named or even felt.
I had always seen him as a figure
whose hands never trembled,
whose thoughts were always guarded,
but today they trembled like leaves in the wind,
like a body reaching for a life that had slipped
beyond its grasp.

He pulled me close,
but the gesture was not one of understanding–
it was something older,
more primal,
as though in that moment,
I had become a reflection of the world
he could no longer navigate.
I wanted to say the words,
the ones that seemed to float above us
like distant, unclaimed ghosts.
I wanted to say,
"I will be better,
I will be the son you imagined I could be,"
but it was useless–
for who could bear the weight of an illusion
that had long been forgotten?

So when they asked me your name,
I wrote God.

Not because I knew who you were,
but because it was the only word
that could encompass
the strange, silent collapse
of everything that was ever true.

29

Scarred/Inheritance

He put down his sword for me–I will not let that surrender go unanswered. Let it be known: I am not here to forgive. I am not here to forget. I was born with his name in my mouth and fire beneath my ribs, and I have carried that heat like a concealed weapon. They mistook his silence for weakness, his dignity for submission, his restraint for defeat. They called him soft because he bled behind closed doors. But I saw it–I saw how he swallowed wars so his children could sleep. I saw how they poisoned him with smiles, how they buried him under the weight of expectations sharpened like spears, how they laughed while dismantling the man who once held up their ruin like a god pretending to be mortal. They thought no one would remember the burn marks he hid beneath his skin. But I was watching. I was learning. I was engraving every slight into the marrow of my becoming.

I am not the son who prays. I am not the son who kneels. I am the son who returns. Who names each scar as a declaration. Who turns silence into artillery. Who answers betrayal not with diplomacy, but with devastation dressed in resolve. Do not speak to me of patience–I have watched it kill the noblest man I have ever known. Do not speak to me of family–he was family, and they made him choke on the word. So let the wind carry this: I am done being still. I am done being civil. I am not here to build bridges over graves. I am the reckoning they buried too early. I am the answer his trembling hands never asked for. And I do not arrive with mercy–I arrive with memory sharpened into edge, with lineage turned to blade. I will not rest until the balance is broken, until their comfort is stripped raw like he was, until every mask is split down the middle by the force of my remembering. He put down his sword for me. I pick it up for him–and this time, it will rain wrath.

30

Reticent

Where does this journey lead, and where am I bound?

In the fragile space between weakness and strength, I find myself lost, adrift in a nightmare of my own mind. A twisted puzzle, a riddle unsolvable, I stagger through the dark, the corners of my thoughts crawling with shadows that whisper false promises of peace. The idea of belonging is a faint memory, a fading ghost that haunts me in my waking hours, always out of reach, like a sickening mirage that vanishes when I reach for it.

Laughter surrounds me–sharp, hollow, mocking–but I am a ghost among the living. I drag my soul through their light, my steps sluggish and weighted with an unseen burden. I am not here with them, never truly here. In the chaos, I lose myself, the roles I play a fragile mask over the abyss within me. I long for sanctuary, a place where the torment might cease, but the very thought of peace twists into something grotesque and distant, slipping further away with each desperate step I take.

I long to be vulnerable, to let the weight that crushes me spill out, but I find no place for it to go. There is no solace. My heart screams for release, but every cry is muffled by the walls I've built. Where is the safe harbour to unearth my soul, to let the darkness inside me finally break free? Is it a curse to remain silent, to bear the heavy chains of my own making? Each moment that passes, I feel myself tightening, bound by invisible ropes, unwilling to surrender to the very release I need.

Each love I carry, I find myself blaming them for the weight I wear. Each one a chain I willingly grasp, a torturous bond that binds me tighter to my own decay. They brush against the surface of my soul, unaware of the horrors festering underneath, the misery that churns and writhes like something alive. I am forced to wear the smile, the mask of joy, while inside, my heart is slowly crushed beneath the unbearable weight of a thousand unspoken sorrows. But who can see? Who can possibly understand the dread I carry?

In their world of noise and comfort, my whispers are drowned, my cries unheard. A silent plea, a guttural scream, lost to the void. Am I a deceiver, wearing the skin of a man while the monster inside gnashes at the bars of its cage? Or is it simply that no one dares to look close enough to see the horror that lives beneath?

Tragedies too vast to comprehend swirl in the recesses of my mind, too monstrous to be spoken aloud. I lock them away, deep in my chest, as if the very act of naming them would unleash the nightmare. Those who love me–they never flinch, never see the terror crawling under my skin. Have I crafted this mask so carefully, built this web of lies so thick, that no one can pierce the veil? Or is it that they are too afraid to look into the abyss?

Is it my own twisted need to hide, to wrap myself in layers of deception, or is it their inability to bear witness to the carnage of my soul?

I long for a moment, just one, where my soul can be seen–not in the shadows, but in the harsh, unforgiving light of truth. I know I am loved, yes–this truth is sharp, unyielding–but should I lock it away, keep it on a shelf, where it is admired but never truly 'felt'?

A love that could heal, yes, but one that I keep locked in a cage of my own design, an artifact of affection I dare not touch. It sits there, just out of reach, its warmth never allowed to burn through the cold of my soul. Should I let it rest, displayed like a trophy, while I continue to suffer in its shadow, never granted the solace it could offer?

And so I wonder, with every passing moment, if hiding it away dulls the pain. Does it sting less, or does the truth–terrible and tender–only wait in the dark, biding its time to shatter the fragile cage I've built? To rise, to tear through the silence, to finally be seen for what it truly is–a nightmare waiting to be realised.

31

Origin (outro)

Life is a brutal battlefield, and you were born into the fire lineage, where struggle is not an obstacle but the very essence of existence. From the moment you drew breath, life has clawed at your peace, testing your every step. Yet, you walked with mercy, though you could have unleashed suffering so fierce that the air would tremble with screams, bones shattering beneath your fists. Instead, you endured the torment of the mind, smiling through the agony, showing the world that your spirit would not break.

This is the strength you were forged in—a fire that taught you to never show weakness, never display fear, even when death itself stalks you, sending tremors through your soul. Courage is not the absence of terror, but the will to push forward despite it. True bravery is feeling the weight of dread yet still stepping into the fight.

It was never about glory—it was about sacrifice. It was never about pride—it was about reverence. It was never about domination—it was about serving the almighty above that rules above all.

You were born to protect, to defend the helpless, and to rise in defiance of what is wrong.

But when you witness the suffering of your ancestors, those who bled and died for this world, only to have it mock their sacrifice, a fire ignites within you. It stirs something savage, reminding you of humanity's bitter, ungrateful nature. Yet, even when your ancestors were battered, broken, and mocked, they chose to honour Maa Bhawani rather than surrender to despair. When you are shattered, when the world thinks it has crushed you, rise again with a fury they will never understand. For when your ancestors gaze down upon you, they will see that though you may fall in battle, you were never truly defeated.

So, when others believe you are on the edge of ruin, rise. Rise and show them the blood that courses through your veins, the purpose that surges through your every movement, the legacy of warriors that you are bound to. Never yield, never bow to their expectations, no matter the cost. Let them feel your strength, let them see that your kindness is a conscious choice, not a flaw, and that spilling blood is not a forgotten myth, but a habit ingrained in your very being. Let them know nothing can break you, Let them know – your origin.

From the world of...

'Healed'

– A compilation of scars

32

More of me

Since you left
I have become more mature,
more practical,
more inhumane,
more arrogant,
more dead,
more of me.
Pain is my ink,
I can't write
if my heart is not sunk into the miseries
I was happy, almost forgotten to write
then you did me a favour
or I did to myself
pushing you away
pushing me to the suffering
I sometimes wonder where was I untrue?
the more I can't find it
the more I find myself close to my pen
I avoid your lanes
keeping close to all pain
they see me the same as they used to
unaware of getting shown, what I choose to
It's so easy to fool people

no one truly knows your third face
undying pain, hidden beneath the jovial maze
I'm exhausted of playing myself
Like I'm not a one-person
Various Roles for various someone
disgusted someone to periyar someone

What's left of me is enough,
enough to gather some strength to pick up the
pen
So I could leash the demons penetrating den
I was –
less mature, more childish
less practical, more jovial
more humane, more kind
more grateful, minimum pride
alive and kicking
that was more of me
which turned into less
and then more into a mess

What you piece by piece tore (out) of me
that was more of me
Now I'm as messed up as this world
and it is on the verge of ending
I'm not sure of me
vented on the wall, cried till fall
then picked up myself, washed up face
to survive and fight –
more of me.

33

A poet's nightmare

12 Dec 2024

Thursday, on a brisk afternoon I witnessed a poet's worst nightmare something which send shivers down to every poet or it is just me, someone tearing apart your poetry, your child, infront of you. something which you nurtured whole heartedly with love, affection, pain, disgust, envy and a little close to death of emotions, something which is you.

I often compare poems to a child and a poet, a mother. I believe the pain it etches your heart when you realise that your child is under the sword because of you. Not every child is same not all of them are great in the societal perspectives but still it's your child.

This time I was not witnessing the nightmare from a mother's eyes, this time I was the pain that was being etched on her child. often being afraid of my child's blood being shed was infact the slayer today. the blood on me hands is still not washed, I still have those stains. Little did I know that for immaterial will I be able to catch a gaze of a mother who saw me slay her child in the vastness of multiple eyes and still couldn't apprehend me for the actions

on this Thursday's afternoon I was the nightmare, which I feared the most, which didn't let me introduce my child to the world with an unhinged introduction that look this is my child and i love him unconditional for who he is. I have not been brave enough with him but I was too cruel with the others' child is the irony and hypocrisy i took home with me, on this Thursday evening.

34

Confessions

Praises, applause, and gentle reminders to *stay good* – that's all a good boy ever receives in his lifetime. Never love, never rage, never even honest hatred. The world keeps its real emotions locked away from him. For the good boy, there are no trembling embraces, no furious passion, no raw humanity – just claps and commands to behave. He walks in the light, yes, but it's a cold light – sterilised, distant – and behind it, a shadow he's never allowed to explore.

These good boys... they live in shallow graves dug by the very hands they trusted. Parents, friends, mentors – they crown him with virtue and then bury him beneath it. And when he sees love – real love, reckless and messy and alive – he doesn't taste it. He watches from a distance, eyes hollow, soul aching, cursing himself for climbing that pedestal. Had he been just a little less perfect, maybe he too could have been human. Maybe he could've made mistakes, broken rules, laughed without apology, cried without shame. Maybe he would've been allowed to fall.

When a failure cries in the corner, someone always comes – a shoulder appears, a hand soothes the pain. But the good boy? He doesn't even dare to sob. He knows what awaits him: not comfort, but correction. Not embrace, but advice. Not love, but lectures. He gets sympathy like charity – shallow and short-lived. The kind that pats your back and pushes you harder the next second.

To the world, good boys are single-use souls – models of morality until they crack. Then, they are discarded, quietly, cruelly. *Use and throw.*

And still, I wish – with every bone in me – that when these boys are chained in obligations they never asked for, something inside them rises. A whisper, a fire, a *no*. Just once. A moment of revolt. To scream. To sin. To say: *enough*. To defy goodness like a rebellion. To bleed and not clean it up. To weep without wiping. To spit on the commandments carved into their backs. To stop being rented hearts for borrowed virtues.

Because this world does not love the flawless. It loves the broken, the loud, the chaotic. Those who falter are the ones who are held. The world says *love heals,* but forgets to ask: who gets loved?

If only the good boy hadn't been wrapped so tightly in perfection, maybe – just maybe – he could've been loved too. Maybe there'd be a soul who could touch his wounds, not just admire his armour. Maybe there'd be a shoulder – not to lean on, but to collapse against. And maybe – just maybe – this world would see that the tears he never let fall, the ones he choked back for years, could drown the very weight it forces him to carry.

35

Heart-bleed

With each passing day,
he saw behaviours tidal –
crashing truths,
receding lies.
Born from a flame himself,
now burning
his own ideals.

He was not made to kneel,
but he bowed–
not to gods,
but to silence.
Not to faith,
but to keep the peace.
A rebel,
not with a cause–
but because.

They told him:
"Grow up, be wise, let go."
But what is wisdom
if not well-decorated surrender?
What is growing up

if not dying creatively?

He carried a heart
too full for rules,
too raw for reason.
And every time he spoke truth,
he paid in blood–
not from his mouth,
but from his soul.

They mocked his fire,
but huddled
when their world grew cold.
They named him mad,
but stole
the heat of his conviction.

He knew –
Rebellion is not noise.
It is ache.
A sacred discontent
that claws from within,
like a lion in a mirror
seeing a sheep's face
and roaring anyway.

This world bleeds
in monochrome,
but he bleeds in colour.
And pain?
Pain is the ink
he tattoos upon fate.

One day,
they'll build monuments
for what they once called madness.
Until then—
he walks,
unloved
but unconquered.

This is heart-bleed.
Not a wound,
but a will.

36

Poet's curse/ Burn me to hell

Poets are fragile, cowards draped in verses. Or is it merely a mirror reflecting my own frailty, my own fear of speaking the truth that festers within me? Is this a curse? Surely, it must be. To bare my soul in ink feels more suffocating than waging a hundred wars. Yes, from where I stand, poets are cowards–weak creatures, mere insects. When faced with the need to step forward, they hesitate, retreating instead into lines of poetry, crafting elegies to their own inaction. They do not fight; they write. They become vessels for borrowed sorrows, architects of laments that mask their failures–their failures in life, in lessons, in love.

Ah, love! What is the worth of weaving words into tragedy when they fail to reach the one who truly matters? Not the world, but *her*. It is not the world that must understand; it is *she* who must know. And yet, this cowardice keeps poets bedridden, drowning in regret, whispering curses upon themselves for letting their beloved slip away. When all that was needed was a letter–not written *for* her, but *to* her.

And then there is *her*–the one for whom the words are spun, who might never read them, or if she does, only when it is too late. And so? At the very least, the poet is left with a wound, not a dagger, bleeding endlessly yet spared from its piercing finality. But if it is truly too late, and she finally reads what was meant for her, let her return it–not with dismissal, but with my heart enclosed, my love entwined, my insecurities stamped, my infatuation sealed, and my feelings carefully wrapped within.

So that when I see *her* again, not in her form but in another, I may have my unbroken self with which to write, my unscorched soul with which to seal, my untouched innocence with which to craft yet another letter–one that, once again, I might send to the world... but never to her.

37

Afterlove

There comes a point when you ask a question so piercing, so uncomfortable, that it shakes the very foundation of your heart: *What lies past love?* It's not just a question–it's a mirror, reflecting everything that once was, and everything that can no longer be. The answer isn't straightforward, nor is it easy. It isn't simply about moving on, nor about staying behind. What follows love, more often than not, is a tangle of things–expectations we never asked for, hopes that cling to us silently, and strangely enough, even the expectation *not* to expect anything anymore. It's like wishing to be free from wishing itself. A strange, looping paradox. We fool ourselves into thinking we can stay in love even after love is gone–but that's not the truth, and perhaps it never was.

In the aftermath, we may still remain in each other's lives, but only in the peripheries. We'll be in touch, yes, but not entangled in the threads of one another's existence the way we once were. We'll still meet eyes across crowded rooms, but the gaze will have shifted. No longer filled with the secrets of shared mischief or silent promises–it will be soft, distant, tinted with empathy, not intimacy. When we cross paths at mutual gatherings, it won't be as lovers or even as former lovers, but as people who merely *knew* each other once–acquaintances who remember too much and say too little.

The occasional message may still be exchanged –brief, courteous check-ins. But the words won't tremble with the weight of unspoken feelings like they used to. That hidden pulse, that quiet longing, will have faded. The subtext will be gone. And when we eventually see each other with someone new, yes, it might sting–but not out of jealousy or lingering love. The pain will stem from a place of gentle concern, like watching someone you once cherished try to build something you no longer have the tools for. Because even though the romantic love between us may have quietly died, the remnants of friendship, or at least care, still linger in the ashes.

And so, when people ask if it hurts to see each other moving on, to watch one another fall into step beside someone else–we'll say no. And we'll mean it, at least partially. We'll smile and nod, pretending the other might be feeling regret, even if we're not. We will put on a face for each other, for ourselves, for the world. It's a strange kind of theatre, this post-love performance.

So once again, we arrive at that first question, circling back like a haunting echo– *What lies past love?* And perhaps the most honest answer is this: *I may not have been enough for you... but I will be enough for myself.* That is the hardest part to accept–that you can love someone deeply, even ferociously, and still find that you no longer *like* them, or no longer like the *us* you once were. It's a bittersweet resignation. Love, it seems, is not always the whole story. Sometimes, the end is not a collapse, but a quiet, necessary letting go.

38

What lies beyond sorry?

Yes, you can strike someone right on their nerves when they are sorry–not with rage, but with a question, quiet and precise, that cuts cleaner than any blade: What lies beyond sorry? It's not just regret–it is the burial ground of intentions, where promises go to die without gravestones. It is guilt that doesn't scream, but whispers persistently in the backdrop of daily silence. It follows like a shadow, always a step behind, reminding them of the moment they became less than who they thought they were. It is not merely the sorrow of the act, but the unbearable weight of knowing they cannot undo its echo. Beyond sorry, there is a detachment that doesn't begin as coldness, but as protection–from themselves, from the weight of being seen again as the person who caused the hurt. It is a self-exile into emotional numbness, not because they don't feel, but because they feel too much, too endlessly, too helplessly.

What lies beyond sorry is the awful clarity that some things, once broken, refuse repair. That words, even if true, arrive as ashes, not balm.

There is care, yes, but it's drenched in helplessness–like hands reaching into water trying to hold a reflection. There is sorrow, but it is hollowed out, ritualistic–more about endurance than healing. And there is humiliation, not public, but private–the kind that eats away at one's self-respect in quiet hours, the kind that makes mirrors unbearable. Sorry becomes a doorway to self-interrogation, not forgiveness. It is a confession without absolution. What lies beyond it is not a bridge, but a chasm. A space where the heart builds its penance, not by pleading, but by remembering–again and again and again. The answer is not a lesson learned, but a scar worn inwardly, a mark that doesn't show, but never stops aching. Beyond sorry lies the acceptance that some things cannot be undone, only carried.

39

More of you

Love is like an unsent letter, it does not vanish; it lingers, like dust in forgotten corners, like echoes in an empty hallway. It does not die but changes its shape–first, a warm embrace, then a distant ache, and finally, an understanding that needs no words. I have watched time stretch and contract between us, moulding you into someone I no longer fully know, yet someone I still recognise in the shadows of my thoughts. You are both familiar and foreign, both mine and unreachable. What once was a shared path has become two roads that run parallel–close enough to see, too far to touch. And yet, there is no tragedy in this. Love, after all, is not possession. It does not require proximity to survive. It endures in fragments–a name I do not say aloud but still hear in my mind, a memory that drifts through my days uninvited but not unwelcome. You exist in the pauses of my life, in the spaces between thoughts, in the silence before sleep. Perhaps love was never meant to be simple. Perhaps it was always meant to be a ghost, haunting and gentle, reminding us of what once was but no longer is.

But if love cannot be reclaimed, neither can it be erased. It lives on, not in the way we had imagined, but in the quiet certainty that if ever asked–more of me or more of you? It has always been more of you.

40

Opinions

I see myself as both absent and present in every atrocity that unfolds, like a silent observer of the chaos around me. I don't truly exist in any real sense; it's merely a mix of fleeting thoughts, blurred ideas, and a chain of opinions that creates the illusion of my being. Inside, I am empty, hollow, my rage evolving into an overwhelming sense of disappointment, a failure to effect any real change. The fire that once fuelled me has dimmed, and now, only anger remains in my eyes, staring at a world that seems unchangeable. I wonder if I'm merely shallow, incapable of feeling anything deeper, or if I've become so broken and reticent that I am beyond repair.

To some, I might appear as one of their own, just another face in the crowd, while to others, I am an enemy, an arch-nemesis even. Some see me as an elitist, disconnected from the struggles of the common people, while others deem me lacking in class or status. Some may even label me as casteist, simply because I challenge the wrongdoings of those on the other side, while my own people turn their backs on me for standing up for what's right. Those who I once trusted as guardians of my ideals have turned out to be nothing more than clowns, masking their true intentions. Meanwhile, those who pose as saviors of the oppressed are nothing but scavengers, waiting for the moment when they can feast on the carcass of a broken system.

The colors of ideologies have blurred and shifted. Saffron has become red, green has grown darker than ever before, yellow has been erased entirely, and white has been repainted a cold, oppressive blue. In this twisted new world, I see black in white and white in black, the lines between what is right and wrong growing more and more obscure. It feels like everyone is putting on a performance, each person playing their part for an audience, driven by a basic survival instinct. Yet, the methods they use to navigate this world have chipped away at the humanity we once held so dear, and now it barely hangs by a thread.

Still, they wear their masks, their hopes for a better year hanging on fragile promises. They gather, they celebrate, they elevate themselves, pretending things will change, but deep down, everyone knows the truth. Nothing will change. One day after another, we continue to live in a state of denial, imitating the rhetoric that our nation is the greatest, but is it really? We are living in a delusion, a carefully constructed fantasy that we all play our part in. The irony is that each and every one of us knows this, yet we still get up every day and play our roles in this farce.

This 'anti-establishment' figure, who once had the strength to speak out, is now too weary to continue calling out the wrongs he sees. This 'anti-national' individual, though labeled as such, loves his country more deeply than anyone can understand, and the 'anti-democracy' person will fight for your rights, even if it costs him everything. Meanwhile, the arrogant man, who may seem callous and self-centered, has always been the kindest at heart. My anger, once so sharp and clear, has slowly melted into disappointment, and so have I. The only emotion I trust now is my rage, because everything else feels like a performance, a facade, a lie.

But what does all this mean to you? Are these just words, a different perspective, the ramblings of someone hopeless and helpless? Or am I just a coward, hiding behind my words? You, too, will wake up tomorrow and play your part in this endless cycle, putting on your mask and pretending for one more day the greatest showman.

And for me, my reflections on a world that seems too broken to fix, too full of illusion to ever be truly real. in other words merely my opinion.

41

Song of love

There are few days when my chest isn't
burdened,
When the weight of stress doesn't constantly
press.
Days when I'd rather write a song of love than a
symphony of emptiness,
When the feeling is not "Phew, it's done,"
But "Oh, goodness!"

Rare days when my smile isn't just a mask of
social pretense,
But a genuine expression of harmony,
A reminder that I too am allowed to feel peace.

But what is a song of love, you ask?
A friend sought the philosopher in me,
But here I am, merely untangling the thoughts
that bind me, Trying to guide myself through the
clutter.

To satisfy curiosity, I answered,
"A song of love is the joy that lifts you up,
But is it truly that?"

No, it is not.

A song of love is when washing dishes feels like
freedom,
When rising from bed doesn't feel like emerging
from a grave,
When my hands are light,
My face unguarded,
My words un-crafted.

It's where I am simply myself,
Letting go,
Not just standing by,
But stepping forward and joining the world.
It's where I'm not afraid to let her see me
As I see myself–

Where my ruthless side makes peace with my
kindness, Where forgiveness comes instead of
revenge, Where bitterness fades, replaced by
tranquility.

That is the song of love,
And today,
I feel like writing one.

42

Symphony of emptiness/ Bloodline

When the song of love is penned,
and the laughter of youthful hearts shatters the
stillness of the room,
we fail to notice how those echoes–so pure, so
wild–
will curl back upon themselves,
silencing the song,
leaving only the haunting symphony of
emptiness.
That silence grows into a chasm,
an abyss that gnaws at the soul,
a rage that stretches like a vast, barren desert,
yet feels more like the suffocating walls of a cage.

Solitude, once a soft refuge,
now smothers,
transforming into the iron grip of loneliness.
The playful scratches of time become jagged
scars, etching themselves deep into the skin of
memory.

The weight of all of it bears down,

a stone pressing into the neck,
a heavy mantle that drags the shoulders to the earth.
And yet, still,
your kindness–   an unbroken thread woven through your veins,
refuses to sever,
because it is who you are,
mad king.
  Mad enough to destroy what lies in your path,
to tear through bonds, relationships,
right and wrong alike,
as if they were nothing but dust beneath your hands.
But still, you wear the crown.

Like your father–
a king whose heart was rich,
but whose hands were weak,
full of tenderness, yet abandoning fury,
breathing in silence,
burying violence beneath the weight of patience.
  You invite the storm,
tread upon fragile threads,
carving pain into your flesh,
yet never surrendering.
Not for glory, not for power,
but for the name that echoes in your blood,
for the shadow of your clan that will never fade.

43

Nocturnal/Nocturne - 1

A mild breeze brushes against my face, its cool touch lightly caressing the nose, now tinged with the soft hue of apricot pink, as the city slumbers in the quiet hours of the night. In the midst of the chaos of life my mind often drifts to the chaos of the day, where I find myself consumed by a relentless tide of thoughts –thoughts that seem to stem from a crisis of identity, thoughts that reflect the infinite possibilities of existence. These thoughts frequently present themselves as the age-old pretext, "Who am I?"–a question that is probably a reminiscent of Nietzsche's challenge to the idea of God, and perhaps to the idea of meaning altogether.

In these small hours, I find a reprieve–a brief escape from the relentless flow of fleeting thoughts, ideas, and inner turmoil. I do not wish for solitude, but the discomfort of standing beside someone who, beneath the surface, feels like a facade is what baffles the outlook to converse and divulge. This paradox makes meaningful conversation seem elusive. I may come across as a hypocrite to many, but is it not the essence of humanity to prioritise practicality over ethics, to seek power over peace, and to evade pain and pursue pleasure?

My texts or poems, whatever you may wish to call them, often seldom revolve around answers they are, instead, a canvas for questions! questions – of existence, of morality, of every necessary evil that is persistent in the contemporary world and which is looked down upon at the very moment it should have been the pulse of the conversation. but if you persist on asking what does these nocturnal hours offer to a mind adrift in confusion – I'd always reply tranquility. they don't ask you to be pretentious, they don't ask you to be on your toes when the world sleeps i can be a little more of myself, I can be with my thoughts a lil more unencumbered by this race of goodness and evil-ry, beyond this world's graciousness and chivalry, no facade or pretentious fences! I can embrace chaos within and let it seep into my senses.

44

Nocturnal/Nocturne - 2

There are moments when the night sky unveils our truest selves, far from the clamour, the noise, and the careless rhythms of others. We are but shadows, draped in pretence, our smiles mere masks that veil the pain we carry–pain that only the stillness of the night dares to expose. From the small hours to the witching hours, we drift in the sorrow of sleep's embrace, some of us sinking deeper, others clinging to the cold wakefulness. In these hours, the ghosts of the past linger, whispering of crises and fractured identities, of the infinite disasters life might unfold. We are haunted by everything we've tried to bury, yet in the silence, we let go of the false selves we so carefully construct, and for a fleeting moment, we are nothing but the absence of noise.

This silence, a haunting lullaby, reassures us–there is life beyond the pretence, a life stripped of chaos and scattered people, a life that hums with peace, though barren of those who matter most, who rarely come. It's in this solitude that I wonder what Premchand might have felt, leaving behind the facade that even Harishankar, who once mocked it, found himself lost in. Harishankar spoke the truth in *'Premchand ke fate joote'* – *"You don't understand the importance of pretence, and here we are, sacrificing ourselves for it."* Pretence is a cruel thing, a poison more bitter than we realise. But what is cruelty compared to the tortured heart of the nocturne, who, sickened by the world's noise, still chooses to embrace the war within—a war that consumes them second by second? They shun sleep, knowing that in these small hours, peace is found only in the silence that devours them whole.

45

Crowned

Often I wonder – what is this world but a theatre of shadows? A grand spectacle staged upon hollow ground, where substance is traded for spectacle, and meaning for mimicry. A masquerade of borrowed purposes, rehearsed ambitions, and desires not our own – where glory is worn like a crown of thorns, bleeding silently into silk. They speak with fervour of greatness, of legacy, of being *seen* – but by whom? A sea of strangers: faceless, transient, forgetful, applauding the echoes of others in a hall lined with mirrors that never reflect the soul.

And yet – there I stood, unmoved and yet complicit, at the very heart of this spectacle I had so vehemently despised. Cloaked in the vanity I once denounced, basking in the glow of eyes I once swore meant nothing. I, who had mocked the altar of fame and ridiculed the worshippers, now knelt before it, whispering my own name in hopes it might echo back. A paradox garlanded in applause – chasing the same hollow recognition I once declared illusion. Is that not the cruelest tragedy? That the seeker of truth – armed with doubt and fire – becomes the servant of delusion, lulled by the sweetness of false affirmation?

Harvey Dent – the caped prophet of modern myth – once warned: *"You either die a hero, or live long enough to see yourself become the villain."* But what if villains aren't born, nor fated – what if they bloom, slowly, in the fertile soil of compromise? In the quiet decay of conviction, and the steady erosion of integrity, do we not build our own masks? Did I act too late? Or – more damning – did I *wilfully* choose inaction? Perhaps my flaws, once repulsive to my conscience, became too applauded to let go. Perhaps the world's claps grew louder than the voice within. My sins began to wear the mask of virtue; my vanity, mistaken for vision. And slowly, I became that which I loathed – not because I failed to resist, but because I *chose* not to.

Maybe I was never escaping the Matrix – maybe I was only refining it, painting its bars gold and calling it freedom. Crafting a more elegant prison, where I could both reign and rot. A throne of mirrors, cold and endless, passed from one reflection to another – each new face cursed with the same old fate. Each condemned, each crowned. Hated, hunted, then hailed – the cycle spins on. The crown falls, only to rise again, reborn upon another weary brow, equally burdened by illusion and performance.

There is no escape. There is no "outside." There is only the play, and we its unwilling actors. Recognition – the final narcotic of the soul – will burn alongside my name. The hunt for glory ends not in revelation, but in ruin. Not in transcendence, but in ash. Only the final fire can silence the applause. Only the pyre can close the curtain on this farce.

Until then, *we dance – crowned, cursed, and clapping.*

AKNOWLEGEMENT

Compiling this book has been an intensely personal journey. The poems within did not arrive in order or form, they came to me in fragments, in scattered pieces. And truthfully, I cannot even claim them as entirely mine. Each line, each emotion conveyed, has been borrowed from the lives around me: from those I hold dear, those I once knew, and even from strangers whose presence left an imprint.

I owe my deepest gratitude to my family– my father, my mother, and my sister– for their boundless love, patience, and support. Much of what I write draws its roots from my upbringing, shaped by the values instilled in me at home.

To my peers, colleagues, and the brothers I found along the way– thank you for not just reading my words, but for believing in them, for celebrating even the smallest moments with me, and for constantly reminding me that my words matter.

A special note of thanks to the vibrant academic tapestry of Campus Law Centre. It taught me that we need not suppress what sets us apart. Rather, we must honour it for it is in our uniqueness that we find our strength.

Finally, to you Mr./Ms. Reader. I hope that within these pages, you discover something of yourself. May you find comfort, courage, and a renewed passion to begin again, especially in those dreams and pursuits you've long set aside.

With warmth and gratitude,
Uday S. Bhadoriya

ABOUT THE AUTHOR

Uday S. Bhadoriya is a writer, researcher, and law student based in New Delhi. He holds a Bachelor's degree in English Literature and Political Science and is currently pursuing his Bachelor of Laws (LL.B.) at Campus Law Centre, Faculty of Law, University of Delhi. He presently serves as the Managing Editor of *CLC-JLPR*, a student-run academic journal committed to legal and policy research.

Hailing from Mauranipur, a culturally rich town nestled in the Jhansi of Uttar Pradesh. He received his early education there, shaped by the ethos and traditions of the region, Uday draws deep inspiration from his roots. Born into a family with deep cultural and historical roots, he was raised with values of discipline and principles that quietly shape both his worldview and his creative work. The rustic ethos of his hometown and the lyrical cadence of the Bundeli language have left a lasting imprint on his soul.

What began as a childhood fascination with history and geopolitics gradually evolved into a deep intellectual affection for political theory and literature. These twin passions now form the bedrock of his writing whether academic or poetic.

This debut collection is not merely a compilation of verses, but a carefully assembled mosaic of memories, thoughts, and borrowed fragments of emotion. Uday writes not to impress, but to connect, to offer readers a moment of stillness, a reflection, or perhaps even the courage to begin again.

धन्यवाद्
Thank You